UNDERSTANDING WEALTH: AND HOW TO GET IT

By

Allen L. Scarbrough, M.B.A.

The richest of men are the quietest.

1.

Wealth has always been a curious word. Whereas money has a clearer definition (anything that can be used as a medium of exchange) wealth has a more ethereal glow. What is wealth exactly? We all (or so I wish) have that rich relation that mother has always called wealthy, but what does she mean? How is wealth determined? That is my task in this little book, to define, explain and elaborate on wealth. Along the way the reader may also encounter a method or two for obtaining wealth. If he or she would like to put these principles to work, they may do so.

Wealth is little more than a store of resources. These resources come in many varieties and can be used in multiple ways. What we call a resource has changed through the millennia. In a hunter-gatherer society where food is not grown, but is plucked up from the good earth, wealth can be anything from fertile soil to brute strength used to wrestle the tastiest morsels from rivals. It could also include access to the most beautiful women for mating purposes.

In the modern world we tend to think of wealth in terms of money. Cold hard cash that can be traded for goods and services. The value of money is negotiable and changes through the years due to inflation, deflation, exchange rates and plain old supply and demand. In years gone by paper money was convertible into a commodity such as gold or silver, but today the value of paper money is determined by the trust in the country that issues it and by buyers and sellers at market. In short, money has whatever value one wishes to place upon it and has no intrinsic value whatsoever. Is this a risky proposition? Yes, in a word. Governmental instability and shortages can wreak havoc on monetary value and countries can reach insolvency in a hot hurry.

So how does wealth enter the equation? Wealth is every resource we have at our disposal for getting gain over others. Today wealth is mostly measured by plain old dollars and yens, but this is not the entirety of wealth. Some resources live in brains in the form of knowledge or creative capabilities. Sometimes this intellectual knowledge can be quantified. For example, authors who have copyright to a series of books often have their future earning potential calculated into their net worth (Harry Potter and J.K. Rowling). A resource can also be the knowledge one has of an industry that would make a return to riches probable should an occasion arise that would wipe out the original fortune. If a man has access to resources, he has the potential to accumulate wealth. Only a prisoner without access to pen and paper or Internet is likely devoid of wealth opportunities though he or she may accumulate barter in the form of cigarettes, provided they do not smoke.

Almost all humans have some inherent value. They can sell their labor in the open market for wages. Indeed, most of us do exactly that. Business owners, entrepreneurs and inheritors are still (and likely always will be) the minority. However, this does not mean that the wage earner cannot become wealthy. It is just a bit harder is all and requires a more restrained obedience to the laws of wealth. In other words, there are fewer methods to become wealthy for those chastened by family and a mortgage.

In the beginning we are all poor. We enter this mortal life with little to show for our efforts. Rather than produce an income we tend to consume the income of our parents. At about age twenty-two to twenty-five we begin our sojourn in the land of money. Some of us arrive with limited resources and some of us come well prepared, but make no mistake, we arrive. Though there are a few that can safely remain within the confines of our ancestral home most of us will be extracted soon enough. We must earn a living and make the bold attempt to accumulate wealth along the way. How is this done?

Many today graduate colleges deep in debt. Student loans are a way to pay for school by using future earnings not yet accumulated. This need not be a source of consternation provided those future earnings are enough to cover the expense of the loan while still living well. A degree in butterfly management with an accumulated debt load of say 80,000 dollars is a recipe for eternal damnation. So before taking out that easy money be sure you are not depending on the crap tables of Vegas for repayment.

Our first job may stink. It may be years before we earn the kind of money we went to college to enjoy, but we can still start the journey in the right way. The first principle of wealth is to begin saving for retirement the day we are born. If that fails, start your 401k the day you start your first job. The law of compounding interest makes it clear that starting early is the way to go. Begun in earnest early in life a 401k can provide a large measure of wealth into old age. With tax advantaged interest a 401k is the surest way to long term security.

Do not make the mistake of waiting until you buy a house or have children to start saving money. I am still waiting to afford children and mine are in their thirties. You can take advantage of many first-time borrower programs to help you get a down payment as well as (if one is lucky) tapping the bank of dad and mom. This leads us to our second discussion question. Should you buy a house or invest the money in blue chip stocks? Let me just say I have seen many blue chips become red chips become nothing while I have seen houses fall down while increasing in value. What do you think?

2.

Real estate is the surest way to accumulate wealth, but it is not as easy as simply buying property. It also includes buying right and knowing the market. Speculation in the real estate market is little better than playing blackjack. The purpose of buying real estate in any market should be first and foremost the collection of rent. Buying assets and then allowing your friends and neighbors to pay for it is an excellent way to wealth. Property tends to increase in value long term due to the shortage of land coupled with a rising population. The old adage "they ain't making any more of it" isn't exactly true, but it works for our purposes.

Most real estate moguls believe you should be flipping houses and/or buying and selling like a wildman, but I am here to tell you this is nonsense. The way to true wealth is to never sell. That's right, you heard it right here. Buy property and never sell it. Instead you will use the equity in your property to finance your lifestyle, buy other properties and to pay for your kid's college. The beauty of living this way, it's tax free. That's right, you pay no taxes on the money you wrestle from your equity and if you never sell you never will pay taxes on that money. Yes, you will pay property taxes, but that will be factored into the rent your tenants pay. Isn't life grand?

In addition to living tax free every improvement in your property increases your equity (provided they are new kitchens, bathrooms and landscaping, not birdbaths) which increases the amount of money that can be borrowed against it. Over fifteen years (never thirty, never ever thirty) the mortgage will be paid off and you will have a lifetime of income to enjoy. Why may you ask, fifteen and not thirty, simple? The cost of a fifteen-year mortgage is only about fifteen per cent higher than a thirty, yet the payoff is half. Equity, which can be borrowed against, accumulates faster which allows the owner to borrow and invest in other properties quicker. Then we sit back and allow the natural economy to wield its mighty sword and wallah, we are eventually quite rich.

The power of real estate cannot be exaggerated. Many businesses use this same formula to become worth millions. They buy commercial property to conduct their business upon then use the cash flow from the business to make the payments and wallah, soon they are quite rich. The smartest businesses never sell the property, but lease it once they are done with it, borrow against the property and buy more commercial property to become even wealthier. It's a beautiful world isn't it?

Let's examine why real estate always goes up in the long run. In the short run there can be market corrections and dips, but in the long run real estate always goes up. Why? As previously stated real estate is a scarce commodity and zoning makes it even more valuable. A city may increase its size by annexing unincorporated areas, but these areas rarely contain much commercial property. The cost of commercial property goes up which in turn makes housing near the commercial district go up and the ripple effect is complete. In addition, wages go up, and the average worker can then afford a larger mortgage payment. The cost of building new goes up, along with wages, making older properties even more valuable, often exceeding the cost of building the property ten or twenty times.

Buying rental property should never come before buying your own personal residence. This is (or it should be obvious) because you must live somewhere and paying rent is a waste of money as your soon to be tenants will attest. Once you have obtained a residence start looking to buy a rental. Take out only fifteen-year mortgages. In a few years, once inflated prices have worked their magic, move up to a bigger home using loans against your equity for a down payment and keep the old place as a wealth building souvenir.

Between your early starting 401k and buying a house and a rental you will be well on your way to wealth, but is this enough? Not quite. There are still other wealth building opportunities at hand. However, I plead with all wealth builders beware of all other ventures because they require the acquisition of more ad more risk and some of us are risk averse, especially spouses.

My parents, middle class at best, began in earnest to acquire wealth by purchasing, and wisely keeping, three properties. They used the buy and hold method described above and it worked. That is until the divorce. So, after thirty something years of marriage they called it quits. The properties were sold and the long decline into near poverty began. These three houses were purchased for a combined sum of 40,000 dollars. The last of the mortgages would have been paid off in 1985. Rents over the last thirty-two years of mortgage free living would have totaled 686,000 dollars and the three properties have a value today of 700,000 dollars.

Assuming taxes and upkeep totaled 186,000 dollars that would have left 500,000 to have been invested in other properties. Assuming twenty per cent down payments and fifteen-year mortgages that money would have purchased approximately two and a million dollars' worth of property. With property inflation and paydowns (some property being bought earlier than others makes this a difficult number to calculate) the estate would now be worth four million give or take. But that assumes no other purchases. If the rental income was continually invested in more properties, the estate could easily be ten to fifteen million dollars. All this off three houses to begin with. Divorce is costly. Since my parents are both dead I would now own this estate and not be writing this book. Intergenerational wealth is a thing people, a real, living thing. Why people insist on buying and selling property is a mystery, it's pure foolishness.

3.

Stocks and bonds are another revenue source, but the odds are good that if you are looking for a quick score you will lose your investment. The best bet here is to invest in mutual funds that minimize (not eliminate) risk. The money used for this purpose should be extra money not immediately needed for other purposes. The best way to invest in stocks and bonds is through a 401k where some risk early in life is tolerable. As one nears retirement this risk should be eliminated, and a fixed return secured. If you feel the need to bet on the next sure thing I suggest the racetrack where at least you get to have a little fun before your money evaporates. Stock purchases are gambling and subject to capital gains taxes. Taxes are bad juju.

Just a note of advice for the parents of twentysomething children, never (and I mean never) tell your kids you have money just sitting around collecting dust. Their devious little minds will think up ways to spend it faster than you can say no. Always reply to a request for funding their sure thing business investment with the following words "I'd love to help you out son (or daughter), but all my money is tied up in investments and I can't touch it for thirty (or however many years you suspect the child might live) years, so sorry. Here's a ten spot for lunch." Sometimes it will be difficult to explain your lack of funds, such as the day your new speedboat arrives in the driveway, but here's how best to explain it to the incredulous child. "It's a bonus from work and after I pay the taxes on it I won't be able to use it much. It's just driveway dressing." And after he or she catches you using it say, "my boss makes me take it out on occasion to justify the bonus and after I pay for gas and oil I can barely afford lunch afterwards." Words like the above can be used for the purchase of any other luxury item. Sear the following mantra into your brain, and I mean really, really burn it in there. Giving money to kids is no better than raking it into a pile and burning it. There, I said it.

Getting back to wealth. Some stupid people say that over the long run stocks outperform real estate. This is statistical manipulation. It assumes, one, that you are in it for the long haul and few ever are, and two, that you never have losses enough to wipe you out. Getting wiped out can take years to recover from and that puts you even further behind in building wealth. Not to mention that stock gains are heavily taxed making any gains negligible expect for that one in a million-crap shoot where a stock goes from five cents to twenty dollars overnight. I personally know of no one who has done this, so I would suggest investing in the lottery instead. Those phenomenal IPO gains you hear about? Rarer than a good T-bone at Denny's. Almost all IPO's lose value over time, if not immediately.

My criticism of stocks does not preclude building wealth that way. You can do quite well in stocks provided you are the CEO of an up and coming company, but if you think about it this amounts to little more than wages over a period of time. Starting a company provides a sense of accomplishment for the five per cent that are still in business after five years. Yes, you heard that right. Ninety-five per cent of businesses fail in the first five years leaving wounds and empty wallets to lick. Leave stocks and bonds for 401k's and invest your spare change in real estate.

What about the billions of dollars Warren Buffet has amassed buying and selling companies. The short answer is he is buying and selling companies not necessarily investing in stock for stock's sake. Mr. Buffet finds undervalued companies with good management and rides them like a pony. In any true sense he is doing with companies what others are doing with real estate. In fact, if you were to look deep into Warrens portfolio you would find that much of the value of the companies he owns is in the real estate they stand upon. Property is power.

Wealth can be built many ways, but if you are poor to begin with the options are fewer. You must acquire assets to become wealthy, indeed, that is the definition of wealth. Starting from scratch means making the necessary sacrifices early on for long term gain. In the short run, only the lotto provides instant wealth and the odds of winning it are slim. In fact, it has been estimated that the average lottery winner is more likely to be struck dead by lightening on the way to pick up their Powerball check than to have won it in the first place, but hey, if you have a spare fiver why not give it a go?

Careful planning will get you there slow and sure. We all want to be rich tomorrow, but there is no lotto in my state and all my older relatives are dead, and broke. So slow and steady it is and I suspect for most of you too. Real estate and a good 401k are the cornerstones of future wealth for most people. Yes, Steve Jobs and Bill Gates became billionaires by starting companies, but in my opinion, they are lottery winners and little else. Someone had to invent the computer age and win out in that business, but it didn't have to necessarily be them. It could have been one of a thousand different people. In fact, Microsoft has made so many mistakes that if they didn't have a monopoly on the windows style of operating system they would have gone under already. Apple almost did go under until the iphone. So, some luck is involved in this type of wealth, just like the lotto or the craps table.

4.

Let us turn our attention to credit for a bit. After all credit is the method by which bankers allow you to purchase the real estate you need to become wealthy. Paychecks come in too slowly for the buying of real estate and in the meantime the ship gets sailed. You will need to build your credit before embarking on the great journey of wealth. So, let's examine how to build your credit and to keep it up. We will want to borrow lots and lots of money, but it must be the right kind of debt. Financing dinner out with credit is dumb, but there are good uses to which credit can be used. Let's start by getting our credit score over seven hundred. And here we go! (Ala The Joker).

A credit score is comprised of several components and knowing how to best manipulate these components will aid us in securing the credit we will need to build our empire. One of the least understood is length of open accounts. Never, and I mean never, close an account. Anyone who counsels you to do this is a moron. The only exception would be an account that charges a large annual fee that you never, and will not ever, use. Length of open accounts is critical because it shows potential creditors that you can pay off debt over a long period of time. Of course, a long period of time must first pass, so when you are getting started open, but never close, necessary credit accounts.

The first item we want is a credit card. Why? Because this is the first step in building credit. In the old days (my day to be exact) credit cards were hard to come by and so often you would have to open a savings account and then borrow against the account to establish credit. This is simply unnecessary today. There was a day when Visa and Mastercard were for the rich alone, but today students will little to no income can open their first accounts while still in school. We want the largest line of credit we can get. Why? Because the larger the line of credit the more we can borrow without tipping our available credit over the twenty per cent level. Keeping your open accounts to a twenty per cent level increases your credit score while having balances over fifty per cent lowers your score. So, longevity and large amounts of available credit is crucial to a high score.

The other main factor should be obvious, pay on time. On time payments raise your score because they indicate an ability to pay. Never forget this, do not ever make a minimum payment, even if it is only a dollar more, pay it. This shows you have loads of cash just sitting around unused. Paying over the minimum not only lowers the amount of interest you will pay but shows creditors you can handle larger credit lines with no sweat.

Lastly, make as much money as possible. This will help you get more credit with larger lines of credit. Believe it or not income is not the be all and end all of credit. I worked in retail for many years and saw thousands of credit applications. A guy making 125k a year would walk in a get an 800-dollar credit approval and grandma, receiving 1400 dollars a month in social security, would get an 8000-dollar approval Why? Good old debt to income ratio. Grandma had no debt and a paid off house. The 125k guy was 300k in debt. So, remember to keep your debt to income ratio low to qualify for more house when the time comes.

Using our established credit, we will next make our first purchase. Hopefully a house, but at least a car. The biggest mistake young people make is buying way more car than they can afford. Everyone likes the new car smell and the idea that no one has driven it before us (though I assure you many lunch runs by employees have already occurred in your shiny new automobile). You can afford a car payment of one half of one week's take home pay. So, if you take home 400-dollars a week you can afford a 200-dollar car payment. This is not going to get you that new Porsche, but it will get you reliable transportation until you are rich. Cars usually depreciate about 40% in the first three years so look for something in that age range to start. If you are lucky and your rich uncle has bought you a set of nice wheels go immediately to step two and buy property. I will go into greater detail about cars in the next section but be advised cars can and will make you poor if you don't watch out.

Establishing credit is essential for achieving lifelong goals. Do not take the advice of some financial idiots and never go into debt. Just make it good debt that furthers your plans and not bad debt like vacations and entertainment. There are wise uses of debt and virtually no rich person gets there without taking on a mountain of debt at one time or another. So, don't be afraid of a little debt, be afraid of foolishness in your financial planning.

I will tackle the issue of student loans in a section all by itself but let me say quickly that this generally counts as good debt. There are interest rate advantages as well as payment plan options that make this a unique form of debt. Just don't go 100k in debt to get a degree in sociology. This degree prepares you only for civil service at low pay. A hundred-thousand-dollar debt for a doctor is perfectly reasonable. However, spending mom and dad's money on college while majoring in partying is by far the best use of parental privilege.

5.

Car, cars, cars. What are we to do about cars? Cars are unique because they look like assets but are in fact expense machines. It is all but impossible to come out on top in the world of cars unless you are a dealer buying and selling them at a profit. However, if you are among the millions of car drivers using transportation to and from work there is no way to use car buying as an investment. Driving is an expense, pure and simple.

The real secret to coming out ahead on cars is to stop driving so much to preserve your car's value. Try shopping online, using public transportation when possible or bumming rides. Driving your car is an expense and expensive. Most modern cars run at about .55 cents a mile, which means when you drive two extra miles to save a buck on a product at the market you lose money. A car is so much more than just gas, there is depreciation, upkeep and insurance to be factored in, not to mention the seemingly eternal car payment. This lack by many people to factor in the full cost of a trip makes for lot of foolish overspending and you never get his money back. Ever.

Try to buy only the size of car you use daily, do not buy something expensive and large for the three times a year you will need it. Pick-ups are by far the biggest squandering waste of all time. For the four or five times a year someone needs one they can be rented at Home Depot for twenty bucks plus gas. This allows you to pocket the extra thirty grand you spent on the monstrosity. If you have a large family and need extra seats there are far better options than a seventy-thousand-dollar Suburban. Use common sense and your needs will be met without the waste of money. Pickups are for business use only.

New versus used. New cars are a good option for leasing, rental car companies and businesses, not for personal use. Yes, somebody must buy new cars for there to be used cars, but let's not make you one of the supreme suckers of all time. Two to three-year-old sedans are the best buy on the market. Sports cars and monster trucks are for the rich. Insurance costs alone will eat you alive with maintenance costs not far behind. Here's why used cars make the best buy.

You read the Wall Street Journal and see that General Motors made a cool billion selling cars last year and you wonder how many cars they had to produce to make that much and the mind reels. The truth? Half of what you pay for a vehicle is pure fluff. A thirty-thousand-dollar car at retail cost approximately fifteen thousand to produce. You, or the supreme sucker if you prefer, pay double the manufacturing cost. The rest is eaten up in profit margins, destination costs, retail markup and unnecessary add-ons. The dealer is not the true culprit. Most of the money goes back to Detroit. So, if you follow the reasoning, the reason a two to three-year-old car is worth half of the cost of a new one is because that is all it was ever worth in the first place. If Walmart manufactured and sold cars a fifteen thousand-dollar car would run you about eighteen grand. Pucker up sweetheart!

For businesses this same scenario does not play out. A business uses a vehicle (or leases) and amortizes the expense on their balance sheet. They will most likely use the full value of the vehicle before trading it in on a new one. Consumers tend to trade in perfectly serviceable cars for no other reason than vanity. Today's modern cars run and run well for 150k or more. Using synthetic oil in the crankcase will make that magic number go up even more. Paint jobs now look shiny and clean for ten to fifteen years. There is no need to trade in a car in under ten years unless you drive excessively.

A word about leases. For private use a lease is a good way to afford more car than you normally would be able to. It essentially spreads out the payments to nine or ten years instead of the usual five or six. Wait, you say, my lease runs three years and I trade it in at the end at a fixed rate. Yes, if you are among the one percent that only drives twelve thousand miles a year. Otherwise, huge penalties are at play at trade in. Most lessees cannot afford to pay those fees and end up buying the leased vehicle for an additional five to six years making the whole painful process a nine- or ten-year ordeal. Whoopee!

The bottom line I that driving I an expense. If you are driving as part of a business where income is produced, happy motoring. If you are driving ten miles to the convenience store because the urge for a soda strikes you at midnight, then I will see you on the poor farm. I live in unit six. Drive when necessity trikes, combine trips, fly when possible do anything but drive your car. Cars have melted away more wealth in America than ten incompetent presidents combined.

In closing this section, I would like to add that buying your child a car is often the best path to long term poverty. Kids don't need cars they need bus passes. If you must, for logistical reasons, buy a kid a car make it the least amount of car you can buy while still having it be safe and reliable. Remember my earlier Mantra, tell kids you are too broke, that your money is all tied up in long term investments, whatever, just do not let them know you can honestly afford anything. One trick I used was to slowly lift a ten-dollar bill out of my wallet making it look as if the act was inflicting actual pain. Never, and I mean never, toss bills out of your pocketbook as if they were made of air. I promise you, your kids will think bills float.

6.

Let us return to making money. With our 401k working and growing, our mortgage getting paid down rapidly, our rentals building equity and our car being rarely used we are on a good path. Is it time yet to build that multi-billion-dollar business idea? Possibly, but caution is required. The best business ideas are the ones that use the talents of the founders to their maximum effect. If it's a service business based on speed of delivery a boss that is efficient is required. The number one reason for business failure (other than stupidity) is pursuing what the business owner perceives is wanted by the consumer rather pursuing a business that inhouse talent can bring to fruition. Bill Gates would have failed miserably at starting a dating website for example.

The great southern general Nathan Forrest Bedford declared that the secret to victory was to get there first with the most men. So, it is also true in business. Ever see those millionaires from multi-level marketing companies declare how easy it was. Well it can be a tad easier for those who got in first. That's where the money is. Businesses have a higher chance of making you rich if you are in on the ground floor than if you come late to the party. Try starting an automobile company today as opposed to the early 1900's. You'll need about three billion dollars to do it right. This might be a challenge on a salary of eighty grand a year. You need to be the first, or at least a very close second, if you wish to get rich in business. And again, as if I need to keep saying it, most of the value of a company is usually its real estate holdings.

I remember my mother working for a real estate firm in Portland, Oregon sometime in the late 1970's when real estate was brutal due to high interest rates. The company had foolishly leased everything from office space to typewriters. When they needed a bank loan to keep afloat they had no assets to borrow against so one of the most promising firms in the area went under. Whether it is business or personal buy and hold assets to get rich.

I also had a friend whose father was a dentist. He wisely built a new dental office with a back office to rent out. In short order the rent on the back office was paying the mortgage while he toiled away in the front office building a small real estate empire. When he retired (at the nice old age of 54) he sold the building at eight times what it had cost to build. Again, he had a profession, but made the bulk of his estate on real estate investments.

Businesses fail. I mean fail, fail. About 95% of all business ventures fail in the first five years. Why? Almost without exception there are two main reasons. Reason one, lack of proper capitalization. Not enough money to begin with to weather the normal ups and down of the business cycle. Reason two, lack of proper management to oversee growth. A lot of businesses do well so long as the principal owners are doing the hands-on day to day, but then they decide to expand and they have to trust others and this only works if proper controls are put in place to prevent the new managers from pilfering the till.

Another word to the wise, if you decide to go into a partnership with anyone (and especially a relative) make sure they pay their taxes (I mean demand to see his or her return) because guess what, you are on the hook if they don't and this has derailed man an exciting new business adventure. Nevertheless, go ahead with your business venture if you are at the forefront of emerging new technologies or have found a new way to market toilet paper, but make sure you have done the steps previously outlined first and make double sure one of you has a real job (if married or domesticated) the cost of health insurance alone might kill you before a disease does.

The truth is only a few precious souls have the talent to pull off a major enterprise. If you are not one of the gifted and have brass balls the size of cantaloupes, I defer you to the age-old method working for someone who does. Riding the coattails of a business genius is better than proving to the world (and your spouse) that you are not. I once knew a young man worth about 150 million dollars. He was succeeding in a business that he had started himself with borrowed money from his father's cronies. However, he had recently failed at his first venture having bet the house money (literally) on the venture. It was a disaster and he had to tell his wife they were broke, but he had a killer new idea that was sure to work. What would my wife say? There's the chicken coop go sleep out there until you come to your senses. However, his wife believed in his abilities and was all in on the new venture which made him wealthy by the age of thirty-five. Lesson here, make sure your partner is on board when you start something new and hide nothing from them. Enough said.

Business is alluring but move with caution. Slow and steady often wins the race. For every Bill Gates and Warren Buffett there is a Harold Steinmetz and a Carol Dimwitty. Ever heard of them? Me neither. But they are well known to their local bankruptcy attorneys. Be first with the most assets, that is my mantra and you will have to borrow lots and lots of cash to succeed so be ready. There is a difference between making an empire and making a living. Some people making a very good living lost it all trying to build an empire. Know thyself, as Socrates said. Are you a Pharaoh or a stonemason, that is the question?

7.

Let us turn our attention to everyone's favorite subject, taxes. Only two things are certain in life, taxes and audits. All our income, investments and even gambling winnings will be taxed in due time. The best bet for wealth building is to pay as little taxes as possible. How is this done without a one ticket to the big house? Planning. Paying taxes without a plan is paramount to using a condom and expecting a pregnancy.

You need to understand the basics. Businesses and real estate have tax advantages others will never enjoy. You can deduct the interest you pay on a property from your taxable income. Though Trump's tax changes have alleviated this advantage for poor people it still works for the well healed. Ah, you say. Those real estate gains you talked about early on will be taxed away as capital gains. The short answer is yes, if you sell investment properties. But remember, we never will. We, the chosen few, will reap even greater reward by continually remortgaging our property and by living tax free off the proceeds. We will also get to deduct all maintenance costs, even those that enhance the value of the property. The government has a strange way of thinking (this is a surprise I bet) they say if you have a duplex and live in one side that that side will stand forever, but the other side will fall down in thirty years. So, we get depreciation along with our deduction for expenses. We are rolling. With our tax-free money, we will build our nest egg even faster.

However, it is important to keep as much of your wages as possible. Mortgages, kids and a hobby business fit the bill perfectly. Don't have any kids? Get going today on a side business. This need not turn a profit in three out of eight years. It is best if you find something that requires a lot of driving as writing off mileage is one of the best ways to avoid taxes. When you turn a profit make it a small profit and when you lose make sure it is catastrophic. Taxes are a necessary evil, but you already pay plenty. You pay at the gas pump, grocery store and the liquor store to name a few. Keep as much of what you make as possible and don't forget the tax advantaged 401K, it's the gift that keeps on giving.

Do your taxes yourself unless you own a full-time business or have just cashed out a million dollars' worth of stock. With tax software (some of it free to lower income people) you can save the fee and put it into savings. As your real estate empire grows you may have need of a CPA, but while you are small do it yourself. New software will aid you in getting every known deduction, some even I wasn't aware of, and help you to pay less tax.

The question of the ages is should you have a lot taken out of your checks and get as big of a refund as possible or figure out your taxes ahead of time and have exactly that amount taken out so you are even at the end of the year. It sounds reasonable to do the latter, but I beg to differ. I prefer the idea of the big refund. Refunds are savings accounts that can provide the down payment for bigger purchases and living month to month on less encourages frugality to make ends meet saving far more money than the interest one pays to the government. And who are we kidding, most of us struggle to save even a few dollars a year. The big refund is a windfall that allows for saving and investing and I embrace it wholeheartedly.

This next item should be self-evident, but in case it is not here goes. When you are paying taxes pay on the last possible day to keep your money in your savings account as long as possible. When you are getting a refund file taxes as soon as the W-4's arrive. You need the money after Christmas anyway. Those idiots standing in line at the post office on tax day are mostly the poor saps who must pay taxes, don't be like them.

Keeping up the Jones will motivate some to overextend. Remember Mr. Jones had an aneurism last year from all the stress and will not live long. Keep your spending to essentials and entertainment. Invest only in things that appreciate, otherwise hold off. You need three televisions like you need a new hole in your head. Make your cars practical and affordable to operate. Buy sturdy furniture that will last and keep your stupid kids off the sofa. You will be able to afford anything you want later on if you follow my plan, but will sink under a mountain of debt and depreciation if you fail to exercise good judgement and self-control.

Now back to taxes. The tax audit is designed to scare the living crap out of you and it usually works, but there is nothing to fear. I have bested the IRS in several hand to hand combats. The secret is to claim an unseen deduction when audited that would make your refund larger. The dillweeds who work for the IRS are scolded for auditing people who are owed more money. Likely, you will never hear from the auditor again. However, if it does come to a showdown pack your weapons carefully and use them wisely. You'll need a good tax attorney if you are a criminal and good common sense if you are not. Remain calm and reasonable. Nutwhackers always look guilty.

8.

Though wealth is our aim we must often be frugal in the beginning. Let's examine what a frugal lifestyle looks like and see how close we can get to living one. The greatest mistake young people make is trying to live like their parents with only a few years of earning under their belts. Swallow your pride and buy that first sofa at Salvation Army and accept hand me downs from relatives, whatever it takes because you need money for investing when you are young more than a new sofa. If you have kids later, they will destroy the first sofa anyway as well as several sets of dining chairs (I speak here from personal experience). Do not buy a pickup. A pickup is the greatest destroyer of wealth among the young. Be frugal and shop sales, shop second hand stores, beg stuff from relatives and parents. The only thing you should spend money on when you are young is buying a house. Always buy the most house you qualify for on a fifteen-year mortgage. Pinch pennies elsewhere. Real estate is your future.

Shopping off season is a good way to pay less. Often retailers are so far ahead seasonally that you can purchase clearance summer items in late august while there are still a couple of months left of good weather. Ditto for winter gear. I once entered a well-known retail store and purchased one thousand dollars' worth of clothes for thirty-five dollars. I went straight to the 90% off rack and found a few treasures then used a twenty dollar off coupon for purchases over fifty dollars and walked out with a full wardrobe for peanuts.

The local dollar tore is another good use of your hard-earned buck. Many products do not require even a Walmart level purchase. There are some cleaning products to avoid, but by and large the local dollar type store will set you up nicely on many items. Some items are much cheaper than retail such as birthday cards and seasonal decorations. I shop my local dollar store regularly and save a small bundle each year. However, a note of caution, Not all items are worth a buck. Candy is often cheaper at Walmart as it is sold at less than a dollar as is the case with several of the liquids the dollar store sells, but shop wisely and you too may save enough for that Italian vacay.

Cable television is another overpriced and expensive luxury. If you have Internet already you are halfway home to saving money. Buy Netflix and Hulu instead. This will cost you about seventeen dollars a month and provide streaming access to most of the shows you watch. Add a Roku device and some of your favorite shows will be live. Roku gives you Fox affiliated networks live and includes the Disney channel, History channel and several more. I find I don't miss cable at all.

Another way to save money is to take a long look at your insurance policies. In general, do not take the advice of an agent. He feeds his family by getting you to purchase unnecessary insurance. Never buy insurance to cover a loss you can easily pay for out of pocket. A lot of people never realize that they have low deductibles on their homeowner's policies that cost them hundreds of dollars a year. You should have no lower than a twenty-five-hundred-dollar deductible for homeowners insurance, anything lower is a waste of money.

Car insurance is another beast that must be tamed. Most finance institutions require a five-hundred-dollar deductible, but if yours doesn't take the one-thousand-dollar deductible instead. There is no reason to make the deductible higher because the savings amount to pennies (don't believe me use the Geico rate calculator and see for yourself). Never, and I mean never, get towing and breakdown coverage through your insurance company, buy it through a third party such as AAA instead. Why? Simple, if you have a claim on your towing coverage through your auto insurance it goes as a claim loss on your report which stays on your record for five years and makes not only your rates go up, but makes it harder to shop for lower rates through other companies. Keep it separate.

Another word to the wise, don't buy extended warranties, as a rule these are a waste of money and only cover the product for the amount of time the manufacturer is pretty certain you won't have a breakdown. This rule does not apply if you are using the product for business purposes. The only product of this type I would recommend is gap insurance on auto financing, especially if you are young. Why? Because when you get hit by someone else it is the insurance company that determines the current value of the car and they tend to be stingy. Also, most people pay too much for new cars in the first place. The gap is the difference between the amount owed on the payoff and the current value which is almost always less than the payoff and guess what, you are responsible for the difference even though the accident is the other guy's fault. I have seen cases where this amount is five thousand dollars or more (yes, I used to be an insurance agent).

Last, but not least, let's consider dining out. Let's exclude the obligatory anniversary dinner and get to the real culprit which is mid-week I'm too tired to cook eat outs. Spending more than twenty bucks for these type meals is a colossal waste of money and it can add up to over a thousand dollars a year easily. Try coupons, sales and plain old bargain hunting when dining out mid-week. Splurging on the occasional four star restaurant is okay now and then but going to anything above a Red Robin or Applebee's mid-week will kill the budget. I recommend eating at home as much as possible, but I am also aware that it gets difficult during a busy week. I save money by having a petite wife who only eats what I would normally put in a box and take home. She's a keeper.

9.

Next, I will speak to the elephant in the room. Okay, now that I've done that let's continue. What is the best way to get the most out of your 401k? The best way is to never, ever touch it. I know that it is tempting once you accumulate a large pile of cash but resist the temptation. The only legitimate use of 401k money is to borrow against it for a down payment on a house. Using hard earned 401k money to finance that once in a lifetime trip to Italy is folly. You cannot afford to go to Italy if you need to tap your retirement funds to do so. This is a rule that can apply to most everything you do.

Should you self-direct your funds? Yes, if your name is Warren Buffett, otherwise no. Why? Because most people who self-medicate have a druggie for a client. The temptation to roll the dice on your future for every whim of easy money is too great. I recommend a medium aggressive mutual fund tapering down to low risk guaranteed income as you approach retirement. This will not save you from the many abuses of the stock market, but it will be better than casting lots to pick your stocks. By the way, ever wonder why we only have recessions now instead of depressions. Easy, because banks no longer have the volatility of days past. Your deposits, up to 250k, are insured so runs on the bank are quite rare, this only leaves the stock market for volatility. Since one leg has been bolstered, we now walk on crutches instead of using financial wheelchairs. If we ever discover a way to insure the stock market, we may just get rich.

Okay, why did we have the great recession of 2007? Because we gave our money over to bandits and then were robbed blind. That simple enough for you? Basically, we made the entire real estate market a giant Ponzi scheme. And when do Ponzi schemes collapse? When they run out of suckers. Once we gave mortgages to hobos and grifters we ran out of potential buyers. We will always have recessions because once an economy gets overheated craziness sets in and we begin to entertain ideas that suck. The recession weeds out these bad ideas and returns us to sanity. So, when you wake up one morning and think, hum, what about a business that takes garbage and turns it into fast food. Know then, my son, we are headed for a market correction.

The real estate accumulation theory of wealth is steadfast and has worked generation after generation. But in reality, any good appreciating asset will work, it's just that there aren't many. Sport teams have historically risen in value, though I think that era is largely past and collectibles, such as art and rarities also rise in value. The value, however, is in the lack of ability to produce more. Art becomes valuable once the artist can create no more of it so the possibility of him or her creating an even better masterpiece than the one you own becomes impossible. The same holds for collectibles, they need to be out of production to have value, otherwise, they just make more of them. I suggest you only use collectibles as a wealth building tool if you have some expertise in that area. A fool collecting coins will one day spend them.

For the vast majority of citizens buying and holding real estate is the only path to wealth. Yes, a 40k can provide a nice retirement, but it is then that you plan to spend it. Few children inherit much of what's left of a 401k especially after mommy or daddy spends the last few years in a home. Real estate can be passed down generation to generation. But I caution you against flipping houses. Yes, a few hardy souls have made money in the short run using this technique, but I again caution you to know what you are doing. It is also possible to lose your entre nest egg on a single bad investment or to get caught with your pants down when the market turns, and you have a five hundred-thousand-dollar albatross hanging around your neck.

The best rental income houses are ones that have been well built in the first place. The better the build the lower the maintenance costs over the long run. Buying a string of throw up houses can bring you to your knees once the first round of replacement costs comes in. Buying slightly older houses with a track record is a safer bet than buying houses in new areas that may yet become disaster areas. Please, please, please check for earthquake and flood history before buying rental property. Buying a lovely little house on the Podunk River may have extra curb appeal, but when the house is seen floating down that same river the rental value collapses. Getting good tenants is a real good idea. If you need to use a property management company do so and remember pets are not allowed in my wealth building scenario.

There are many pitfalls of wealth accumulation, but only a few tried and tested means to building wealth. I'm sure that new methods will arise in future days, but for now buying and holding appreciable assets is the most common. Anything that is consumed is wealth eating, anything that sits there and doesn't do much is wealth building. Food, clothes, cars and vacations consume wealth. Houses, businesses, art, collectibles and land build wealth. Delayed gratification also comes in handy, but few possess the ability to lay off the Twinkies.

10.

In this last section (yes, all good things must end), I will go over the fundamentals of wealth creation one more time and add a few more words of caution. One of the best predictors of future production is past production (though there are a few exceptions). Real estate over the last six thousand years of civilization has been the most proven and productive creator of wealth. Who was the richest man in Rome? Marcus Crassus. And how did he get so rich? Real estate, primarily apartment complexes. Though it is rumored Markus had a few of his apartments burned down for the insurance money he still used the surest method of wealth accumulation. While others mined stone quarries or sold fine linens or even made war materials good old Markus Crassus out earned them all. Yes, he was killed by having molten gold poured down his throat by barbarians, but what a way to go.

In the modern world wealth has also been created by conquering the digital world. Microsoft, Apple, Google and Amazon have used computers and the Internet to build vast fortunes, but in this game there are usually only a small handful of winners and a whole lot of losers. In the game of life, we all want to be winners, right? Real estate is the surest bet for the common man to rise above his station, that and winning the lottery.

So, let us go over the fundamentals one more time. First get an education or at least some form of technical training. Get a job, start your 401k as soon as possible (never touch it) and buy your first home immediately and shortly thereafter your first rental property. Then you are well on your way, but I can't stress enough the importance of starting early. If you are thirty and still living in your parent's basement the ship has already sailed on your future. Get out there and make it happen.

Life is what happens when you're busy making other plans, according to John Lennon (he was a Beatle for you young folk). Unfortunately, most of us lie awake at night dreaming of a magical future that will not happen unless we make it happen. Following a time-tested formula will work better than an incomplete and ill-conceived dream. Buying and holding real estate and other appreciable assets will make you richer than dreaming of winning the lottery (few do and those that do often lose their money within five years).

Starting young allows the time value of money to work it's magic. So powerful is the time value of money that if the Indians had invested the proceeds from the sell of Manhattan (estimated at thirty-four dollars) in a simple savings account paying an average of three per cent the account would now be worth two trillion dollars, talk about getting rich! Build intergenerational wealth, not just a nest egg for your own use. This is how empires get built. Real estate is the cornerstone of any good venture. Even if you pursue business make sure you buy the property your business uses as that will likely become most of the market value once the technology catches up to your venture.

Never stop looking for your next score. Having sold real estate myself for a time I learned that the best properties rarely get listed. Instead, they sell so fast there isn't time. Befriend realtors and bankers for leads on the best deals. And remember, if you slightly overpay time will make up your loss. Appreciation will swallow your overpricing and still make you rich in the long run. Life is an amazing journey, but you travel so much better with money in your pocket.

Never underestimate the value of a good spouse. You are in this journey together and must make decisions together. If you marry someone overly timid about money you will likely never have much money to argue over. Make sure you are both on the same page. If you choose to reman single your journey can still be prosperous, but it will take longer for those whose incomes are under 100k a year. And, by all means, take time to smell the roses. Hopefully these will be roses resting in a flowerbed you own. Never leapfrog your income. Spend as you go and never make luxuries needs. We need transportation, food, housing and clothing, but we don't need the best of everything at the first. Too many young people strive to keep up with parents that have been working for twenty to thirty years. This is a mistake. Remain humble until circumstances improve. Controlling yourself if as important as controlling your money. If you are using luxuries to make up for deficiencies in other areas, you will fail to accumulate wealth.

Finally, not all wealth can be counted. Do not forget the pleasures of children and grandchildren and spending time with them. There are many joys and pleasures that cost little. Walking on the beach, laughing with a grandchild or taking a country drive. Not everything of value can be purchased with money. Money is the engine that drives the world, but happiness drives the driver. We are here on earth for only a brief instant. Life goes quickly so the time is now to implement your wealth building plan. There is no time to lose. Even if you are older and have missed other opportunities many more opportunities still exist. Seize the day!

Make happiness your goal and wealth your hobby, a singlemindedness on more can lead to early death and a joyless life. Remember there are other aspects of life worth pursuing other than building wealth, but if you use the principles outlined in my little book you can achieve both happiness, fulfillment and monetary security. To be happy is to bless the world. Find your bliss and life will unfold its treasures unto you. Here's to your future wealth and having it all. Good advice, I think.

www.ingramcontent.com/pod-product-compliance
Lightning Source LLC
Chambersburg PA
CBHW030514220526
45464CB00006B/2798

LA CHIMIE ET L'ENVIRONNEMENT

CE QUE VOUS DEVEZ SAVOIR

(QUESTIONS ET REPONSES)

By Rumi Michael Leigh

Introduction

Je tiens à vous remercier et à vous féliciter pour l'achat de ce livre "*la chimie et l'environnement, ce que vous devez savoir (questions et réponses)*".

Ce livre vous aidera à comprendre, réviser et à avoir une bonne connaissance générale et des mots clés de la chimie et l'environnement.

Encore merci d'avoir acheté ce livre, j'espère que vous l'apprécierez !